IN THE COURT OF APPEAL OF THE STATE OF CALIFORNIA

FOURTH APPELLATE DISTRICT, DIVISION TWO

I0481585

Salvatore A. Buono

    Petitioner and Appellant

v.

Carolyn N. Beggs

    Respondent and Respondent

Court of Appeal No. E066816

(Super Ct N. SWD003122)

Appeal from a Judgement

Of the Superior Court, Country of Riverside

Hon. Judge F. Paul Dickerson

———————————————

APPELLANT'S OPENING BRIEF

———————————————

Salvatore A. Buono

20845 Sylvester Road

Lake Elsinore, CA 92530

(714) 356-5366

Appellant

Self-Represented

TABLE OF CONTENTS

TABLE OF AUTHORITIES

CASES

BOOKS

STATEMENT OF THE CASE

The Petitioner-Appellate Salvatore Buono and the Respondent Carolyn Beggs (formerly Buono) were married on July 27, 1997 [CT 232] and had one child Matthew Buono, born Sept. 28, 2003 [CT 5]. The dissolution of marriage was filed Jan. 20, 2004 [CT 402]. The final judgment, was issued May 19, 2005 [CT 429], but was not signed until Mar. 28, 2006 [Augmented Record 124]. The final judgment states in relevant part that,

> "The PETITIONER shall continue with supervised visitation with a professional monitor, until such time as he petitions the court for any and all changes and until such time as he completes all of the requirements as set forth in the previous mediation." [Augmented Record 127].

The previous mediation took place on Sept. 2, 2004, and included only two requirements [Augmented Record 22];

- First, Mr. Buono was to complete co-parenting parts A and B [Augmented Record 23], which he completed on March 15, 2005 [Augmented Record 121].

- Second, Mr. Buono was to complete any needed repairs to the family residence [Augmented Record 23]. However, Mr. Buono never owned the family residence, so Mr. Buono built a brand new home in June 2005 [Augmented Record 130].

In Aug. 2005, Mr. Buono appealed the unsigned May 2005 order [CT 436], the appeal was dismissed Oct. 12, 2005 [CT 437]. In April 2006, Mr. Buono appealed the signed March 28, 2006 judgment [CT 439], the appeal was affirmed Jan. 3, 2008 [CT 470]. On Sept. 11, 2007, Mr. Buono was declared a vexatious litigant [CT 466], Mr. Buono appealed, but abandoned the appeal and it was dismissed Dec. 6, 2007 [CT 470].

In Nov. 2007, the Court Mediator recommended unsupervised visitation, but Ms. Beggs contested [Augmented Record 142:11-27], her attorney Mr. Cohen stated,

"...Is that we really think there should be some type of psychological testing of the petitioner. ... before we move to the nonmonitored. Again, we read in the papers scary things daily, and we've seen enough strange and bizarre conduct in this particular case .... And we would propose that, one, if the Court wants to set this for hearing, we'll bring in this document and my client will authenticate..." [Augmented Record 145:24-28, 146:1-8].

Therein, Judge Codrington ordered a 730-evaluation [Augmented Record 149:20-26], two Trials, and an interim custodial order. To recite Judge Codrington,

"...But I'd like to schedule the evidentiary hearing on custody and visitation at the same time as the hearing on the evidentiary issue regarding the document that was attached to the respondent's declaration." [Augmented Record 150:5-11]. "... As an interim order I would like to increase that time..." "And I see by your reaction, ma'am, you don't want to increase the time, but I am staying the unsupervised visits and giving Father up to 12 hours per week," [Augmented Record 153:5-7, 153:27-28, 154:1].

However, at the Oct. 28, 2008 Trial, Commissioner Bermudez made the most critical of errors, as Commissioner Bermudez claimed that the evidentiary hearings ordered by Judge Codrington had already been denied, appealed, and affirmed. To recite Commissioner Bermudez;

> "I scratch my head, gentlemen, because it appears that Judge Codrington in 2007 ruled that there weren't any change circumstances. Her ruling was challenged. The Court of Appeals sustained her ruling, so I wonder if there are any changed circumstances even in the pleading that are before me. … you would have the burden to tell me your changed circumstances." [CT 324:17-25].

Mr. Buono attempted to correct Commissioner Bermudez's misconception. Attempting to explain that the Final Judgment was Temporary, and that Judge Codrington's Orders were Temporary [CT 325:7-13, 326:1-2]. While simultaneously Ms. Beggs' attorney Mr. Cohen seemed to increase the confusion. To recite Mr. Cohen;

> "Not only are we post, that was already modified once so we aren't even looking to modify the judgment. There was an order subsequent to the judgment." [CT 325:26-28]. "I understand what the Court's read. Mr. Buono immediately filed a post-judgment modification of custody and visitation based upon that …" [CT 326:20-22].

Mr. Buono even tried to explain that because his Motion only sought a modification of visitation, not a change in custody that he was <u>not</u> required to show a change of circumstances [CT 325:14-17].

To recite Mr. Buono;

"Since then, Your Honor, the appellate court ruled that a change of circumstances is not the appropriate standard. It is the best interest of the child standard. And so since I'm asking for a modification of visitation, not a change in custody, I only need to meet the best interest of the child's standard, and I've had two separate evaluators, one in 2007 and one in 2008, recommend that visitation be modified to take me off of supervised visitation." [CT 327:18-26]

Thereafter, Commissioner Bermudez's made these comments and dismissed the case;

"For the record, number one, as I indicated in my opening comments to both of you gentlemen, it seems to me this issue has already been addressed not once but twice. Both times no change were found. I would be prepared to find there aren't changed circumstances at this point warranting a revisitation of the parenting time between the parties. Even assuming arguendo that the standard of review for me is the best interest of the child and [assuming] that I would revisit custody under that standard, I am prepared to find that no modification of the orders in terms of parenting time between father and child is in the best interest of the child.'"" [CT 334:3-14].

Additionally, Commissioner Bermudez, on the court's own motion, ordered a restraining order for the child Matthew [CT 321:8-15]. Mr. Buono appealed, the appeal was denied [CT 493]. However, the child's restraining order has since been defeated and removed [RT 3:8-14].

7

At the Aug. 4, 2016 Hearing, Mr. Cohen began by misrepresenting the Supreme Court Law. Specifically, Mr. Cohen claimed;

> "The law is clear. The Supreme Court has made it very clear that before this man could come in and request a modification of the visitation, he has to show and demonstrate substantial changes in circumstances which would warrant a modification of -- of the visitation." [RT 5:1-5]

The distinction may seem subtle, but Mr. Buono's motion specifically requested only 12-hours of unsupervised visitation with supervised exchanges [CT 172:6-10]. Mr. Buono filed the Full Opinion *in re the Marriage of Lucio, infra*, [CT 127-137], which explains that the noncustodial parent who is seeking only a modification of visitation time without a change in parenting time is not required to show changed circumstance [CT 127-137].

Second, Mr. Cohen misrepresented the court's proceedings. To quote Mr. Cohen;

> "Not only have we gone to Trial in 2006, but then due to numerous filings by this individual, a 730 was finally ordered." [RT 5:6-7].

Again, Mr. Cohen had requested the 730 in 2007 because there are scary things written in newspapers [Augmented Record 145:24-28, 146:1-8]. In fact, the (2008) 730 and the 2016 Report both recommended unsupervised visitation with a step-up plan [Confidential Material Transcript 118-119] [CT 372-373].

Thereafter, to recite Commissioner Dickerson findings;

"Okay. Just listen. I think the point of Mr. Cohen is -- at the end of the day is, Judge, we're

post-judgment. It's a Montenegro order. There is no material change of circumstances. ... I

just agree with Mr. Cohen. -- this case goes so far back ... So it's an old case. I can't go back

and rehash 13 years of history. I can only rule on what I have today, and I just don't find a

material change of circumstances. There is no change. [RT 12:15-27].

Finally, as noted, Mr. Buono was declared a vexatious litigant [CT 466], so Mr. Buono was not

allowed to represent himself. However, Mr. Buono's motion specifically requested only 12-hours

of unsupervised visitation with supervised exchanges [CT 172:6-10]. Mr. Buono argument cited

in re the Marriage of Lucio, infra, [Augmented Record 162-169], which explains that the

noncustodial parent who is seeking only a modification of visitation time without a change in

parenting time, is not required to show a change of circumstances [CT 127-137]. Further, while

seeking equal justice and uniformity of law, Mr. Buono cited four 2010 through 2014,

unpublished opinions, including Riverside County, Sacramento County, and San Diego County

Appellate District Courts all citing and agreeing with Orange County's 2008 finding *in re

Marriage of Lucio, infra* [Augmented Record 163-166]. However, Commissioner Dickerson

denied that motion for reconsideration without allowing a hearing [Augmented Record 170].

STATEMENT OF APPEALABILITY

This appeal is from the judgment of the Riverside County Superior Court and is authorized by the California Code of Civil Procedures, §904.1(a)(2).

STATEMENT OF THE FACTS

At the first mediation, March 15, 2004, the Respondent Carolyn Beggs (formerly Buono) requested that the Petitioner-Appellant Salvatore Buono be placed on supervised visitation, Ms. Beggs alleged that the couple's former home was in disrepair and unsuitable for a child, Ms. Beggs also claimed that Mr. Buono threatened to kidnap their child. Additionally, Ms. Beggs admitted that she was physically abusive toward Mr. Buono during their marriage [Augmented Record 11].

Mr. Buono explained to the mediator that he had his own daycare center which was located within his sister Francine's home. Mr. Buono cited that he was already caring for two other children, and Mr. Buono stated that he wanted to care for their son Matthew at his sister Francine's home. Additionally, Mr. Buono was concerned about Ms. Beggs' drinking problem [Augmented Record 11].

The mediator recommend that Mr. Buono would care for their child during Ms. Beggs full work day, Mondays through Fridays and that Mr. Buono would have alternate weekends, allowing Mr. Buono a 50/50 share [Augmented Record 14-15]. But at the Mar. 23, 2004 hearing, <u>Ms. Beggs had the daily visits reduced</u> to only 9:00AM until 1:00PM, Mondays through Fridays [Augmented Record 15].

On July 29, 2004, <u>without personal knowledge</u>, as Ms. Beggs was not present for the exchanges, Ms. Beggs filed an ex-parte <u>falsely</u> accusing Mr. Buono of being tardy when dropping their child off at the KinderCare daycare center [CT 13:12-19]. Specifically;

1. Ms. Beggs claimed that on June 2, 2004 that their child was returned 50-minutes late [CT 13:26]. However, subpoenaed daycare records revealed a return time of 12:50 [CT 27], which was 10-minutes early.

2. Mr. Beggs claimed that on June 7, 2004 that their child was returned 35-minutes late [CT 13:27]. However, subpoenaed daycare records revealed a return time of 12:35 [CT 28], which was 25-minutes early.

3. Ms. Beggs claimed that on June 16, 2004 that their child was, again, returned 35-minutes late [CT 14:1]. However, subpoenaed daycare records revealed a return time of 12:35 [CT 28], which was, again, 25-minutes early.

4. Ms. Beggs claimed that on June 18, 2004 that their child was returned 60-minutes late [CT 14:2]. However, subpoenaed daycare records revealed a return time of 1:08 [CT 30], which was 8-minutes late.

5. Ms. Beggs claimed that on June 22, 2004 that their child was returned 40-minutes late [CT 14:3]. However, subpoenaed daycare records revealed a return time of 12:40 [CT 31], which was 20-minutes early.

6. Ms. Beggs claimed that on June 23, 2004 that their child was returned 60-minutes late [CT 14:4]. However, subpoenaed daycare records revealed a return time of exactly 1:00 [CT 32], which was exactly on time.

7. Ms. Beggs claimed that on June 24, 2004 that their child was returned 55-minutes late [CT 14:5]. However, subpoenaed daycare records revealed a return time of 12:55 [CT 33], which was 5-minutes early.

8. Ms. Beggs claimed that on July 8, 2004 that their child was returned 1-hour and 10-minutes late [CT 14:9]. However, subpoenaed daycare records revealed a return time of 1:12 [CT 35], which was 12-minutes late.

From Mar. 23, 2004 through July 29, 2004, Mr. Buono had returned their son 107-times, this is computed by counting the dates on the calendar. If we subtract the 8-false late dates listed in Ms. Beggs' affidavit, then there are at most 5-late drop-offs within her complaint [CT 14:6-14]. Further, Ms. Beggs also falsely inserted an additional hour into each of those late drop-off dates. For example;

9. Ms. Beggs claimed that on July 9, 2004 that their child was returned 1-hour and 30-minutes late [CT 14:10]. However, subpoenaed daycare records revealed a return time of 1:30 [CT 36], which was 30-minutes late.

Additionally, Ms. Beggs admitted that she had authorized some afternoon visits when she needed to take the child to a morning doctor's appointment [Augmented Record 19:21-28, 20:1-12]. However, there was a dispute over which of the 4-late dates were authorized by Ms. Beggs. For example;

10. Ms. Beggs claimed that she authorized an afternoon on April 19, 2004 [Augmented Record 20:7-9]. However, subpoenaed daycare records revealed a return time of 1:15PM and that Matthew remained in daycare until closing at 6:30PM [CT 39].

11. Ms. Beggs claimed that Mr. Buono had violated the court order on July 12, 2004, by returning their son 3-hours and 20-minutes late [CT 14:11]. But, Ms. Beggs also claimed that she had authorized an afternoon visit on July 13, 2004 [Augmented Record 20:11-12]. However, subpoenaed daycare records revealed a return time of 11:30AM and that Matthew remained in daycare until closing at 6:30PM [CT 43].

At Trial, <u>KinderCare daycare employee Pamela Lee testified that Ms. Beggs had misrepresented the child's daycare return time</u> as 11:30 to 12:00 noon [Augmented Record 53:7-11]. Further, Pamela Lee testified that Mr. Buono had explained that his return time was actually 1:00PM [Augmented Record 54:16-25].

However, at the July 29, 2004 ex-parte, the Family Court reduced Mr. Buono's visits from 26-days of visits per month to just Alternate Weekends [Confidential Material Transcript 98]. A change from joint custody to visitation at an ex-parte.

At the Sept. 2, 2004 mediation, the mediator recommended that Mr. Buono be placed on supervised visitation until he makes repairs to the family residence [Augmented Record 23]. Specifically, Mr. Buono stated that after his custodial time was reduced that he had moved back into the allegedly unrepaired family home, but that he was still caring for their child Matthew at Francine's house during his alternate weekend visits [Augmented Record 22]. However, Ms. Beggs "suspected" that Mr. Buono was secretly bringing their child to the allegedly unrepaired home [Augmented Record 22].

Thereafter, at the Sept. 8, 2004 hearing, the Family Court placed Mr. Buono on family supervised visits and appointed Mr. Buono's sister Francine as the supervisor [Augmented Record 23].

On Dec. 15, 2004 Ms. Beggs filed an ex-parte, the ex-parte was denied, however, at the Jan. 25, 2005 hearing Ms. Beggs was granted a restraining order. Ms. Beggs gave two different versions of the alleged Nov. 26, 2004 Event;

1) In Ms. Beggs' Dec. 7, 2004 version of the Nov. 26, 2004 Event, Ms. Beggs stated that she had reconciled with Mr. Buono [CT 141:4-23] and Ms. Beggs' attorney Mr. Cohen stated that the reconciliation lasted for "four days" approximately two weeks prior to the Dec. 7, 2004 custodial hearing [CT 141:20-23]. Mr. Cohen also admitted that Ms. Beggs had been allowing Mr. Buono to receive the child unsupervised [CT 143:14-17].

Please note that the custodial order granted Mr. Buono both Thanksgiving Day and the 48-hour alternate weekend Friday Nov. 26 through Sunday Nov. 28, 2004 [Augmented Record 15]. We can verify the alternate weekend by noting that Mr. Buono also had another alternate weekend Friday Dec. 10 through Sunday Dec. 12, 2004 [Augmented Record 68:10-16].

2)   In Ms. Beggs' Dec. 15, 2004 version of the Nov. 26, 2004 Event; Ms. Beggs claimed that Mr. Buono had allegedly forcibly taken their child from her car, and then demanded that Ms. Beggs follow behind him in her own car [CT 51:22-26], under threat that Ms. Beggs would never see her child again [CT 52:3-8]. Ms. Beggs stated that she stopped following Mr. Buono and called the police [CT 52:7-10].

Further, at the Jan. 25, 2005 hearing, Mr. Buono argued that Ms. Beggs' and Mr. Cohen's failure to reference this so-called "child kidnapping" at the Dec. 7, 2004 custodial hearing, was in itself evidence that these events had not occurred. As was the fact that Ms. Beggs could not produce a police report [Confidential Material Transcript 114, 115] [CT 287:6-25]. However, in an inappropriate act, Ms. Beggs' attorney Mr. Cohen lied to the Family Court, falsely claiming that they had reported these allegations within the Dec. 7, 2004 hearing [Augmented Record 35:9-21] and the Family Court granted Ms. Beggs' restraining order.

Clearly, a comparison of the Dec. 7, 2004 transcript [CT 139-144] with the Dec. 15, 2004 affidavit [CT 45-53] would have revealed Mr. Cohen's deception.

On Jan. 6, 2005 Ms. Beggs filed another ex-parte, this time Ms. Beggs claimed that Mr. Buono had returned their child one day late after the 2004 Christmas visitation [CT 59-69];

It should be noted that there was a mistake in the custodial order that gave Ms. Beggs both Christmas Eve and Christmas Day for EVEN YEARS [Augmented Record 15], and that Mr. Buono had attempted to correct this error on Dec. 7, 2004, and that the Family Court had verbally granted Mr. Buono 8:00AM Christmas Eve until 12:00 noon Dec. 25, 2004, but nothing was put in writing [CT 143:9-19].

First, Ms. Beggs falsely claimed that the Family Court had only granted Mr. Buono visitation from 6:00PM Dec. 24, 2004 until 12:00 noon Dec. 25, 2004 [CT 63:5-12]. Ms. Beggs then admitted that she had refused to release the child to the supervisor Francine at the court ordered 8:00AM, forcing Francine to wait until 6:00PM [CT 63:22-25].

Second, Ms. Beggs admitted that on the morning of Dec. 24, 2004, that Mr. Buono had telephoned Ms. Beggs, to quote, "On Dec. 24, 2004, I received a telephone call from the Petitioner in the morning." [CT 63:27, 64:1].

However, at Trial;

- Mr. Buono asked, "Do you remember Mr. Buono calling you on Christmas eve, December 24th, 2004?" And Ms. Beggs answered, "You didn't call me. You called my mother in the morning. You called my mother." [CT 299:6-9].

17

- Mr. Buono asked, "And did I speak to you?" And Ms. Beggs answered, "You did not speak to me. You spoke to my mother." [CT 299:10-11].

- Mr. Buono asked, "So in this affidavit you say that I received a telephone call, meaning yourself, Ms. Beggs, are you saying that that was a mistake?" And Ms. Beggs answered, "I didn't receive a phone call. My mother received the phone call at 8:00 o'clock in the morning." [CT 299:12-16].

- Mr. Buono asked, "Did you receive a phone call at 9:00 o'clock in the morning?" And Ms. Beggs answered, "I didn't receive a phone call. You did not talk to me." [CT 299:17-20].

Third, Ms. Beggs' affidavit claimed that on Dec. 24, 2004 (Christmas Eve), that Mr. Buono had allegedly gone to Ms. Beggs' place of employment, to quote; "On Dec. 24, 2004, I received a telephone call from the Petitioner in the morning. He stated that he was calling the police. He thereafter came to my place of employment at Robinsons-May and wouldn't leave until security forced him to leave." [CT 63:27, 64:2-8].

Mr. Buono subpoenaed the Robinsons' May security records for Dec. 24, 2004, which showed that store security was never called and that there was no such incident [CT 146].

Additionally, at Trial, Mr. Buono posed the following question;

- Mr. Buono asked, "Ms. Beggs you also stated Mr. Buono came to your work on December 24th, 2004; is that correct?" Christmas Eve. [CT 294:22-24].

- Ms. Beggs' attorney Mr. Cohen stated, "I believe that misstates the evidence, Your Honor." [CT 294:25-26].

- And Ms. Beggs answered, "No. You did not come to my work Christmas eve." [CT 294:27-28].

Fourth, Ms. Beggs stated that the child had been "essentially kidnapped" [CT 64:22-25]. Ms. Beggs expressly stated that she called both the supervisor Francine's and Mr. Buono's cellphones [CT 64:13-15]; In contrast, Francine's subpoenaed cellphone records (#3.002) and Mr. Buono's subpoenaed cellphone records (#3.003) showed no in-coming calls from either Ms. Beggs or the maternal grandparents [Augmented Record 93:5-27, 108].

Fifth, Ms. Beggs alleged that the police were called not once but multiple time [CT 64:16-18] [CT 65:13-14]. However, Ms. Beggs admitted that the police never ordered an Amber Alert (Amber Alerts were Established in California on July 24, 2002). No arrest. In fact, Dr. Suiter's 730 cited that Ms. Beggs had no documentation to support any of her claims, not even a simple police report to show that she had even called the police [Confidential Material Transcript 109, 114, 115] [CT 287:6-25].

Further, Mr. Buono specifically questioned Ms. Beggs at Trial, about the existence of this "police report," specifically;

- Mr. Buono asked, "And have you filed any police reports with this court to support what you claim?" Ms. Beggs answered, "I filed my restraining order with the police departments, Mr. Buono." [CT 287:6-9]

- Mr. Buono Asked, "But did you file a police report when you called the police? In any of these situations did you file that police report with this court? Ms. Beggs answered, "No. I did not file the police report with the Court because the police had already made a report." [CT 287:10-14].

- Mr. Buono asked, "Did you have the report printed out from the police station and bring it to the Court and file it with the court so the judge could see it?" Ms. Beggs answered, "No. I went to my attorney." [CT 287:15-18].

- Mr. Buono asked "Ms. Beggs, did your attorney file a police report with this court?" Ms. Beggs answered, "I'm not aware of that, Sal. You need to ask him." [CT 287:23-25].

Nonetheless, at the Jan. 6, 2005 ex-parte, no police report was required, the family Court placed Mr. Buono on Professionally Supervised visitation at 6-hours per week and Mr. Buono has remained on professionally supervised visitation for the past 12-years [Augmented Record 28:4-24].

The only significant question relating to parenting at the May 2005 evidentiary hearing, is whether the then 14-month-old Matthew was injured while in Mr. Buono's care. Specifically; on Jan. 25, 2005, Ms. Beggs claimed that Mr. Buono had returned their child in a horrifying condition, to recite Mr. Cohen;

"If the court wants to see the condition of the child when the child is returned from this person, I can show you pictures. I think the mediator saw these as well. It is horrifying."

At the May 2005 Trial, the maternal grandfather William Beggs testified that he had taken photographs of the child on Sunday Dec. 12, 2004 shortly after the child was returned [Augmented Record 68:10-16]. William Beggs stated that he thought that Matthew was a "little bit bruised." [Augmented Record 69:19-22]. In dispute, Mr. Buono argued that the pictures were fakes [Augmented Record 30:9-13, 96:17-18].

- Mr. Buono subpoenaed the KinderCare daycare record for Monday Dec. 13, 2004, which showed that the child Matthew had <u>no injuries on Dec. 13, 2004</u> [Augmented Record 122].

- Mr. Buono subpoenaed the KinderCare daycare employees, wherein Pamela Lee testified that there were no significant injuries, and that injuries are brought to the attention of the parents [Augmented Record 29:10, 53:15-28, 54:1-4].

- Further, Mr. Buono subpoenaed the Thursday Nov. 11, 2004 KinderCare daycare record which showed that Matthew had scratches to his knees and legs on Thursday Nov. 11, 2004 [Augmented Record 123]. It should be noted that Mr. Buono's supervised visitation stated at 5:00PM Friday Nov. 12, 2004 [Augmented Record 15].

The final judgment was issued May 19, 2005 [CT 429], but was not signed until Mar. 28, 2006 [Augmented Record 124]. The final judgment states in relevant part that,

"The PETITIONER shall continue with supervised visitation with a professional monitor, until such time as he petitions the court for any and all changes and until such time as he completes all of the requirements as set forth in the previous mediation." [Augmented Record 127].

The previous mediation took place on Sept. 2, 2004, and included only two requirements [Augmented Record 22-23];

- Mr. Buono was to complete co-parenting A&B [Augmented Record 23], which he completed on March 15, 2005 [Augmented Record 121].

- Mr. Buono was to complete repairs to the family residence [Augmented Record 23]. However, Mr. Buono never owned the family residence, so Mr. Buono built a brand new home in June 2005 [Augmented Record 130].

Thereafter, on Nov. 8, 2007, Ms. Beggs rejected the mediator's 2007 recommendation for unsupervised visitation [Augmented Record 142:11-27], And Ms. Beggs' attorney Mr. Cohen argued that,

"…Is that we really think there should be some type of psychological testing of the petitioner. … before we move to the nonmonitored. Again, we read in the papers scary things daily, and we've seen enough strange and bizarre conduct in this particular case that I think this absolutely warrants being as cautious as we can with this minor child. And we would propose that, one, if the Court wants to set this for hearing, we'll bring in this document and my client will authenticate and go through it; and, two, that there be some type of psychological testing of the petitioner," [Augmented Record 145:24-28, 146:1-8].

Therein, Judge Codrington ordered a 730-evaluation [Augmented Record 149:20-26] Two Trials, and a Temporary Custodial Order. To recite Judge Codrington;

"I am not going to consider those notes for today's hearing because they have not been presented to me in an authenticated form. So we will have to deal with that when we have the hearing. But I'd like to schedule the evidentiary hearing on custody and visitation at the same time as the hearing on the evidentiary issue regarding the document that was attached to the respondent's declaration." [Augmented Record 150:5-11].

"… As an interim order I would like to increase that time…" "And I see by your reaction, ma'am, you don't want to increase the time, but I am staying the unsupervised visits and giving Father up to 12 hours per week," [Augmented Record 153:5-7, 153:27-28, 154:1].

Dr. Suiter's (April 2008) 730-Psychological Evaluation found some disturbing issues relating to Ms. Beggs. To recite Dr. Suiter's Report;

"[Ms. Beggs] completed the Personality Assessment Inventory. The profile was valid. The results were reflective of an individual likely experiencing a very heightened degree of anxiety even to a degree which is unusual for clinical samples. As a result, her life is likely to be severely constricted by her tension and she may even be unable to even met minimal role

23

expectations without feeling overwhelmed. In that regard, relatively minor stressors for her may be sufficient to result in a major crisis as she is prone to be plagued by worry making it even difficult to concentrate." [Confidential Material Transcript 110, 111]

"[Ms. Beggs] stated she considers there needs to be continued supervised visits of their son with Mr. Buono until their son reaches the age of eighteen. When asked the reason for that she stated because Mr. Buono is not "mentally stable" and that he is a "mentally ill." When asked to define his mental illness, she stated that she believe he has "some form of autism or Asperger's." When asked even if that were true how that would necessarily negatively impact upon his ability to care for their son, she stated that such a disorder "might interfere." She then stated that Mr. Buono is a "psychic medium" [Confidential Material Transcript 108-109].

"Lastly, [Ms. Beggs] asserted that Mr. Buono had attempted to obtain a Passport and had intent to abduct and had even once "Kidnapped" their son. However, she provided no documentation to support that he had applied for a Passport for their son. She provided no documentation that he had ever been arrested specific to abducting their son. Nor did she even provide a police report to indicate that she had made a report to that effect.
[Confidential Material Transcript 114-115].

Dr. Suiter's 730-Psychological Evaluation recommended that Mr. Buono be taken off supervised visitation, and that Mr. Buono be placed on a step-up plan [Confidential Material Transcript 118-119].

To recite Dr. Suiter's Report:

"In total, the data from the evaluation did not support that their son is at any risk towards being with his father. Indeed, it was noted that the child is very warm and responsive to his father and very definitely wanted to be with him…" [Confidential Material Transcript 115].

"Further, the data does not support that he presents a risk to their son. Rather, [Mr. Buono] is likely to be quite appropriate with their son and to be focused on their son's well being. He is likely to be warm and nurturing with him as well. He is likely to engage him in age and developmental appropriate activities and is unlikely to be harsh with any disciplining." [Confidential Material Transcript 116].

"As Mr. Buono was observed as he went to retrieve Matthew it was noted that Matthew very readily and eagerly went to his father. There was certainly no hesitation at all. As they entered this examiner's office, they brought in a number of action figures they played with on the carpet. Mr. Buono engaged Matthew in a fantasy game with the figures, although as if they were a family and trying to find treasure. Mr. Buono was very warm, interactive, and quite animated with his son. Matthew was very responsive to his father and clearly enjoyed being with him. There was no indication at all that Matthew was in any manner uncomfortable with his father or hesitant with him. Indeed, Mr. Buono had no difficulty at all maintaining his attention." [Confidential Material Transcript 113].

However, at the Oct. 28, 2008 Trial, Commissioner Bermudez made the most critical of errors, claiming that the Evidentiary Hearing(s) ordered by Judge Codrington had already been denied, appealed, and affirmed. To recite Commissioner Bermudez;

> "I scratch my head, gentlemen, because it appears that Judge Codrington in 2007 ruled that there weren't any change circumstances. Her ruling was challenged. The Court of Appeals sustained her ruling, so I wonder if there are any changed circumstances even in the pleading that are before me. He would have the burden to tell me there are – well, actually in terms of this, you would have the burden to tell me your changed circumstances. Why am I revisiting these orders?" [CT 324:17-25].

Mr. Buono attempted to correct the misconception. Attempting to explain that the Final Judgment was Temporary, and that Judge Codrington's Orders were Temporary [CT 325:7-13, 326:1-2]. While simultaneously Ms. Beggs' attorney Mr. Cohen seemed to increase the confusion. To recite Mr. Cohen;

> "Not only are we post, that was already modified once so we aren't even looking to modify the judgment. There was an order subsequent to the judgment." [CT 325:26-28]. "I understand what the Court's read. Mr. Buono immediately filed a post-judgment modification of custody and visitation based upon that …" [CT 326:20-22].

Thereafter, the Commissioner made these comments and dismissed the case;

"For the record, number one, as I indicated in my opening comments to both of you gentlemen, it seems to me this issue has already been addressed not once but twice. Both times no change were found. I would be prepared to find there aren't changed circumstances at this point warranting a revisitation of the parenting time between the parties. Even assuming arguendo that the standard of review for me is the best interest of the child and [assuming] that I would revisit custody under that standard, I am prepared to find that no modification of the orders in terms of parenting time between father and child is in the best interest of the child."" [CT 334:3-14].

Additionally, at the Oct. 28, 2008 hearing, Commissioner Bermudez, on his own motion, ordered a restraining order for the child [CT 321:8-15] and a 52-week anger management for Mr. Buono [CT 323:19-21]. However, the child's restraining order has since been defeated and removed [RT 3:8-14], the anger management completed [RT 8:14-17].

Most Recently:

Mr. Buono has been held under professional supervisor for 12-years now. Yet, Mr. Buono has maintained regular weekly visits [Confidential Material Transcript 367]. These visits span thousands of hours all successful and uneventful [Confidential Material Transcript 366-370].

In contrast, the professional supervisor's incident report revealed several disturbing issues regarding Ms. Beggs. For example the report states;

"9/13 Minor child reported an incident that had occurred between himself and the custodial parent. Minor child stated that the custodial parent had punched him in the face during an argument that occurred in the front yard. The minor child was crying as he relayed this incident to the non-custodial parent. He stated that the custodial parent had told him that someone was coming to investigate the incident and he was scared that he might be taken away." [Confidential Material Transcript 370].

In dispute, Ms. Beggs stated,

"I believe that he is an habitual liar. I have never punched my son in the face. [CT 340:6-9].

Further, Ms. Beggs entire comment was,

"I believe that he is an habitual liar. I have never punched my son in the face. I am not aware of any neighbors seeing this or calling CPS on me. I have not had any visits from CPS in this regard." [CT 340:6-9].

However, the court evaluator in 2015 discovered that there had been 9-mandated calls to CPS against Ms. Beggs [Confidential Material Transcript 364-365]. Mandated calls are calls from teachers or other government officials who are required by law to report signs of neglect or child abuse.

Again, Ms. Beggs admitted to a history of being physically abusive toward Mr. Buono during their marriage [Augmented Record 11].

The professional supervisor's incident report also stated that,

"There have been times when the minor child has stated anger with the custodial parent, however he had not gone into detail. He states that the anger management that he has had in school has helped. He also states that he will be going to regular classes next year." [Confidential Material Transcript 370].

Further, before the child's restraining was removed, the professional supervised witnessed Ms. Beggs allowing Mr. Buono unsupervised visits. For example;

- In Aug. 2013, the professional supervisor noted that approximately 40-minutes after the supervised visit had ended, that she received three phone calls from Mr. Buono and the child Matthew, over a 2-hour period. Wherein Matthew explained that his mother Ms. Beggs was outside talking, while Mr. Buono and Matthew were inside playing video games [Confidential Material Transcript 369].

- In June 2012, the professional supervisor noted that after Mr. Buono's supervised visitation had ended that the professional supervisor witnessed Ms. Beggs walking hand in hand with the child, back into the restaurant where Mr. Buono was having his daughter's birthday party [Confidential Material Transcript 369].

- Also, in June 2012, the professional supervisor noted that Ms. Beggs attended Mr. Buono's daughter's birthday party. That Ms. Beggs sat at the same table as Mr. Buono, that Ms. Beggs sang happy birthday, ate cake, and watched Mr. Buono's daughter opened presents [Confidential Material Transcript 369].

- In April 2012, the professional supervisor noted that Ms. Beggs attended a movie with Mr. Buono and Matthew [Confidential Material Transcript 369].

It should be noted that Ms. Beggs denied drinking and passing out in front of the child [CT 340:10-11]. However, the child never accused Ms. Beggs of drinking in front of him, but rather, the child stated that Ms. Beggs had been 'sick' and 'hung over' [CT 172:13-14]. Noting that Court Orders had stated that Ms. Beggs was not allowed to drink alcohol in front of the child [Augmented Record 16].

Additionally, the mediator's 2016 report recommended unsupervised visitation and a step-up plan [CT 372-373], which was similar to Dr. Suiter's 2008 recommendation for unsupervised visitation and a step-up plan [Confidential Material Transcript 118-119]. Mr. Buono cited that he had remarried 9-years ago, that Mr. Buono has raised a second child, who is now 7-years old. That Matthew is well-bonded with both his step-mother and his sister [Augmented Record 166:24-28].

Lastly, please note that Mr. Buono was declared a vexatious litigant [CT 466], so Mr. Buono was not allowed to represent himself. However, Mr. Buono specifically requested only 12-hours of unsupervised visitation with supervised exchanges [CT 172:6-10]. Mr. Buono filed the Full Opinion *in re the Marriage of Lucio, infra* [CT 127-137], which explains that the noncustodial parent who is seeking only a modification of visitation time without a change in parenting time, is not required to show a change of circumstances [CT 127-137]. Further, Mr. Buono made his Best Interest of the Child arguments clear by citing the *Marriage of Lucio, infra,* and several other Best Interest cases within his written arguments [Augmented Record 162-169].

However, to recite Commissioner Dickerson;

"… this case goes so far back … So it's an old case. I can't go back and rehash 13 years of history. I can only rule on what I have today, and I just don't find a material change of circumstances. There is no change." [RT 12:15-27].

I. Is a Significant Change in Circumstances required when modifying a Visitation Order (Parenting Time) from Professionally Supervised to Unsupervised visits without a change in custody?

De Novo Standard of Review:

Since this issue involves the superior court's interpretation of the "Change of Circumstances" rule, without a factual analysis, the reviewing court should determine whether the trial court's interpretation was proper and legal based upon the "De Novo" standard. Pure questions of law are reviewed de novo. *(See People v. Cromer (2001) 24 Cal.4th 889, 894 citing Pullman-Standard v. Swint (1982) 456 U.S. 271, 289 [72 L.ED.2d 66, 102 S.Ct. 1781].*

Legal Argument:

"[T]he changed circumstance rule does not apply when a parent requests only a change in the parenting or visitation arrangement not amounting to a change from joint custody to sole custody, or vice versa. Instead, the trial court considers a request to change the parenting or visitation arrangement under the best interests of the child standard." *(In re Marriage of Lucio (2008) 161 Cal.App.4th 1068. 10811082.).*

"The changed circumstance rule applies to a modification request seeking a change in a final determination of custody. The changed circumstance rule does not apply to a modification request seeking a change in the parenting or visitation schedule. *(Enrique M. v. Angelina V. (2004) 121 Cal.App.4th 1371, 1379-1380, 18 Cal.Rptr.3d 306 (Enrique M.); In re Marriage of Birnbaum (1989) 211 Cal.App.3d 1508, 1513, 260 Cal.Rptr. 210 (Birnbaum).)* In Birnbaum, the mother contended the trial court erred by granting the father's request for a modification of the parenting and visitation schedules in a joint custody arrangement without requiring the father to demonstrate changed circumstances. *(Birnbaum, supra, 211 Cal.App.3d at p. 1513, 260 Cal.Rptr. 210.)* The Court of Appeal, affirming, held the changed circumstance rule does not apply when an order does not change custody but only alters a parenting schedule. The court stated: "The basic deficiency in [the mother]'s contention and her appeal from an order she claims changes custody is, whether there were changed circumstances or not, there has been no change of custody. The trial court ordered, 'The parties shall continue to have and share joint legal and joint physical custody of their minor children,' just as they did under the prior order. At most there has been a change in what the trial court deemed the 'co-parenting residential arrangement.' " (Ibid.)

In Enrique M., the Court of Appeal held the trial court erred by applying the changed circumstance rule to deny a father's request to alter a visitation schedule in a joint custody arrangement. *(Enrique M., supra, 121 Cal.App.4th at p. 1373, 18 Cal.Rptr.3d 306.)* The Court of Appeal concluded the changed circumstance rule does not apply to requests for modification of parenting or visitation arrangement not amounting to a change in custody. *(Id. at pp. 1373, 1382, 18 Cal.Rptr.3d 306.)* In reaching this conclusion, the court noted the "California Supreme Court has repeatedly discussed the changed circumstance rule in cases involving requests to modify custody, where granting the request would remove custody from one parent and give it to the other parent." *(Id. at p. 1379, 18 Cal.Rptr.3d 306.)* After discussing Birnbaum, the court concluded that case and the Supreme Court decision in *In re Marriage of Burgess (1996) 13 Cal.4th 25, 51 Cal.Rptr.2d 444, 913 P.2d 473* (Burgess) were consistent. *(Enrique M., supra, 121 Cal.App.4th at p. 1380, 18 Cal.Rptr.3d 306.)*

This recognition that a trial court has residual and broad discretion to modify visitation orders led the Enrique M. court to conclude Burgess was consistent with Birnbaum. The Enrique M. court explained: "The Burgess court's statement that a trial court has the discretion to modify visitation orders, without any suggestion that the noncustodial parent would have to demonstrate changed circumstances to justify such changes, is fully consistent with Birnbaum. Further, the Burgess court's statement that such modifications of visitation could serve to obviate time-consuming custody litigation illustrates the distinction between requests to modify visitation, or parenting time, and requests to modify custody." *(Enrique M., supra, 121 Cal.App.4th at p. 1381, 18 Cal.Rptr.3d 306.)*

The father in Enrique M. requested an alteration in the parenting schedule to give him, each week, one extra overnight with the child and an additional overnight every other week. *(Enrique M., supra, 121 Cal.App.4th at p. 1382, 18 Cal.Rptr.3d 306.)* The Court of Appeal stated, "[a]lthough [the father]'s proposed changes would alter the parenting schedule, in terms of potential instability for [the child], they were not on par with a request to change physical custody from sole to joint custody, or vice versa." (Ibid.) Because the father did not seek to modify custody, the Court of Appeal concluded the trial court erred by applying the changed circumstance rule. (Ibid.) The court reversed because the trial court had stated it would have reached a different result under the correct standard. (Ibid.)

Birnbaum, Enrique M., and Niko concerned requests to change a parenting or visitation schedule in a joint custody arrangement, while in this case, Ms. Beggs had sole physical custody of the child. The reason for not requiring a showing of changed circumstances is equally applicable to a request to alter the visitation schedule when one parent has sole physical custody. In Enrique M., the court explained the changed circumstance rule is based in part on the need to protect stable custody arrangements believed to be in the child's best interest. *(Enrique M., supra, 121 Cal.App.4th at p. 1382, 18 Cal.Rptr.3d 306.)* The changed circumstance rule promotes such stability "by preventing the reexamination of final judicial determinations of custody in the absence of 'some significant change in circumstances.' " (Ibid.) Unlike a change in custody, an alteration in a parenting or visitation schedule does not cause a disruption in "established patterns of care and emotional bonds with the primary caretaker" *(In re Marriage of Brown & Yana, supra, 37 Cal.4th at p. 956, 38 Cal.Rptr.3d 610, 127 P.3d 28)* justifying the added burden of demonstrating changed circumstances." *(In re Marriage of Lucio (2008) 161 Cal.App.4th 1068. 10811082.)* [CT 130-133].

In our case, Mr. Buono's OSC sought 12-hours of unsupervised visitation with supervised exchanges [CT 172:6-10]. Noting that Mr. Buono already had 12-hours of professionally supervised visitations [Augmented Record 153:5-15]. And that Mr. Buono has been consistently visiting their son for over 12-years, with all visits being successful and uneventful [Confidential Material Transcript 366-370].

Therein, Mr. Buono was not seeking additional time with his child. He seeks merely an adjustment in the terms of visitation. The only change that will result from the court's order is that Mr. Buono will be able to visit his child alone, without the intrusion of expense of a third party supervisor.

"Unlike a change in custody, an alteration in a parenting or visitation schedule does not cause a disruption in "established patterns of care and emotional bonds with the primary caretaker'" [citation] justifying the added burden of demonstrating changed circumstances." *In re Marriage of Lucio (2008) 161 Cal.App.4th 1068, 1079 (Lucio); see also Enrique M. v. Angelina V. (2004) 121 Cal.App.4th 1371, 1379-1380; in re Marriage of Birnbaum (1989) 211 Cal.App.3d 1508, 1513.).*

Mr. Buono's requested alterations to the existing parenting and visitation schedules would not have created a de facto joint custody arrangement. *(See In re Marriage of Biallas (1998) 65 Cal.App.4th 755, 760, 76 Cal.Rptr.2d 717* [when father has right to visit on alternate weekends and one weeknight each week, custody was not joint custody].) The requested alterations would not disrupt the children's established patterns of care and emotional bonds with Ms. Beggs or destabilize the sole physical custody arrangement. As in Enrique M., Mr. Buono's proposed changes to the visitation schedule, though altering the parenting schedule, were not "on par with a request to change physical custody from sole to joint custody, or vice versa." *(Enrique M., supra, 121 Cal.App.4th at p. 1382, 18 Cal.Rptr.3d 306.)*

It should be understood that Mr. Buono was originally placed on Family Supervised Visitation on Sept. 8, 2004, because Ms. Beggs, "suspected" that Mr. Buono was secretly bringing their child to the allegedly unrepaired home [Augmented Record 22-23]. And that this became Professionally Supervised Visitation after Ms. Beggs claimed that Mr. Buono had returned the child one day late after the Christmas 2004 visitation.

Specifically, there was a mistake in the custodial order which gave Ms. Beggs both Christmas Eve and Christmas Day for EVEN YEARS [Augmented Record 15]. Mr. Buono brought the error to the attention of the Family Court and the Family Court issued a verbal correction [CT 143:9-19]. However, Ms. Beggs incorrectly recorded the court adjusted time schedule [CT 63:5-12]. As a result Ms. Beggs had the child for Christmas Eve [CT 63:22-25] and Mr. Buono had the child for Christmas Day [CT 64:12-13, 65:16-19]. Ms. Beggs argued that this act was a short period kidnapping and that their child was in danger [CT 69:3-5]. Thereafter, at the Jan. 6, 2005 ex-parte, the family Court placed Mr. Buono on Professionally Supervised visitation at 6-hours per week.

However, none of Ms. Beggs allegations were ever proven. The May 19, 2005 Court Order, signed Mar. 28, 2006, stated in relevant part;

"The PETITIONER shall continue with supervised visitation with a professional monitor, until such time as he petitions the court for any and all changes and until such time as he completes all of the requirements as set forth in the previous mediation." [Augmented Record 127].

The previous mediation required nothing more than that Mr. Buono was to complete co-parenting and to make repairs to the family home [Augmented Record 22-23], and Mr. Buono built a brand new home in June 2005 [Augmented Record 130].

Thereafter, in Nov. 2007, the Court Mediator recommended unsupervised visitation, but Ms. Beggs contested [Augmented Record 142:11-27], her attorney Mr. Cohen stated,

"…Is that we really think there should be some type of psychological testing of the petitioner. … before we move to the nonmonitored. Again, we read in the papers scary things daily …" [Augmented Record 145:24-28, 146:1-8].

Therein, Judge Codrington ordered an interim custodial order, pending the 730;

"… As an interim order I would like to increase that time…" "And I see by your reaction, ma'am, you don't want to increase the time, but I am staying the unsupervised visits and giving Father up to 12 hours per week," [Augmented Record 153:5-7, 153:27-28, 154:1].

And, Dr. Suiter's (2008) 730-Psychological Evaluation recommended that Mr. Buono be granted unsupervised visitation and placed on a step-up plan [Confidential Material Transcript 118-119]. To recite Dr. Suiter's Report:

"In total, the data from the evaluation did not support that their son is at any risk towards being with his father. Indeed, it was noted that the child is very warm and responsive to his father and very definitely wanted to be with him…" [Confidential Material Transcript 115].

But, at the Oct. 28, 2008 Trial, Commissioner Bermudez made the most critical of errors, incorrectly claiming that the evidentiary hearings ordered by Judge Codrington had already been denied, appealed, and affirmed [CT 324:17-25]. As a result of Commissioner Bermudez misconceptions, the case was dismissed leaving Mr. Buono on Judge Codrington's Nov. 2007 interim order, forever.

And most recently, the 2016 court mediator recommended unsupervised visitation and a step-up plan [CT 372-373]. Wherein, the 13-year-old Matthew also requested unsupervised visits [RT 3:12-13]. And, Commissioner Dickerson made no comments on the issue of Child's Best Interest, but rather, he stated that

"… If you're post judgment, and we are post judgment from 2008 – I am showing March 28th, 2006, when it was filed – you have to show a material change of circumstances before you get anywhere else [RT 9:24-28, 10:1]. "…I can't go back and rehash 13 years of history." [RT 12:24-25].

Therefore, Mr. Buono would request that the Appellate Court reverse and remand with a finding that the Family Court used the wrong standard of review. That the correct standard was the Best Interest of the Child Standard. Further, to find that this issue has merit, such that Mr. Buono would be allowed to represent himself on remand.

II. **Did the Family Court Error in Finding that the Modification of an Interim Custodial Order Required a Showing of a Change of Circumstances?**

Abuse of Discretion Standard of Review

In general, "[t]he standard of appellate review of custody and visitation orders is the deferential abuse of discretion test." *(In re Marriage of Burgess (1996) 13 Cal.4th 25, 32 (Burgess).)*

"Under the changed circumstances rule, after the trial court has entered a final or permanent custody order reflecting that a particular custodial arrangement is in the best interest of the child, custody modification is appropriate only if the parent seeking modification demonstrates ' "a significant change of circumstances" indicating that a different custody arrangement would be in the child's best interest.' " *(In re Marriage of Lucio (2008) 161 Cal.App.4th 1068, 1072.)* Our Supreme Court has explained that rule "fosters the dual goals of judicial economy and protecting stable custody arrangements" and is " 'based on principles of res judicata.' " *(Burchard v. Garay (1986) 42 Cal.3d 531, 535.)*

In contrast, at "an initial custody determination, the trial court has 'the widest discretion to choose a parenting plan that is in the best interest of the child.' [Citation.] It must look to all the circumstances bearing on the best interest of the minor child." *(In re Marriage of Burgess (1996) 13 Cal.4th 25, 31-32; see In re Marriage of Brown & Yana (2006) 37 Cal.4th 947, 955-956.)*

Therefore, a party seeking to change an interim or temporary custody order would an easier burden than a party seeking to change a final or permanent custody order. *(See, e.g., Christina L. v. Chauncey B. (2014) 229 Cal.App.4th 731, 738* [improper modification of final order where trial court did not require movant to show changed circumstances]; *In re Marriage of McLoren (1988) 202 Cal.App.3d 108, 116* [similar holding]; *cf. Keith R. v. Superior Court (2009) 174 Cal.App.4th 1047, 1053-1054* [improper for trial court to require movant to show changed circumstances, when no prior final judicial custody determination had been made].)

In determining whether a custody order is a temporary or final order, The sole trigger is whether the order sought to be modified was intended to be a 'final' judicial custody determination—without regard to whether it was entered after a contested hearing or by default judgment or by stipulation. *(3 Hogoboom & King, Cal. Practice Guide: Family Law (The Rutter Group 2015) Modifications of Orders and Judgments, ¶ 17:298, p. 17-98; see Montenegro v. Diaz (2001) 26 Cal.4th 249, 257-259 (Montenegro); In re Marriage of Richardson (2002) 102 Cal.App.4th 941, 951-952.)*

The sole trigger is whether we are trying to modify a custodial order that was issued with the intent of being the final custodial determination. This means that if we had a final order, we'd have a judge who believed that they were issuing the final order.

In our case;

1) On Aug. 4, 2016 Commissioner Dickerson stated;

"... It's a Montenegro order. There is no material change of circumstances. ... I can't go back and rehash 13 years of history. I can only rule on what I have today, and I just don't find a material change of circumstances. There is no change." [RT 12:15-27].

Thus, by the sole trigger argument, Commissioner Dickerson's was not trying to issue a Permanent and Final order structured in the child's best interest. But rather, he believed that there was already such a Final Order in place. .

2) On Oct. 28, 2008 Commissioner Bermudez stated;

"I scratch my head, gentlemen, because it appears that Judge Codrington in 2007 ruled that there weren't any change circumstances. Her ruling was challenged. The Court of Appeals sustained her ruling," [CT 324:17-25]. "For the record, number one, as I indicated in my opening comments to both of you gentlemen, it seems to me this issue has already been addressed not once but twice. Both times no change were found. I would be prepared to find there aren't changed circumstances at this point warranting a revisitation of the parenting time between the parties." [CT 334:3-14].

Thus, by the sole trigger argument, Commissioner Bermudez's was not trying to issue a Permanent and Final order structured in the child's best interest. But rather, he believed that there was already such a Final Order in place.

3) On Nov. 8, 2007, Judge Codrington stated;

"…But I'd like to schedule the evidentiary hearing on custody and visitation at the same time as the hearing on the evidentiary issue regarding the document that was attached to the respondent's declaration." [Augmented Record 150:5-11].

"… As an interim order I would like to increase that time…" "And I see by your reaction, ma'am, you don't want to increase the time, but I am staying the unsupervised visits and giving Father up to 12 hours per week," [Augmented Record 153:5-7, 153:27-28, 154:1].

Judge Codrington specifically stated that she was issuing an "interim order," pending a Trial. Hence, Judge Codrington did not intent to issue a Permanent and Final Order.

4) The May 19, 2005 Final Judgment, signed On Mar. 28, 2006, in relevant part states;

"The PETITIONER shall continue with supervised visitation with a professional monitor, until such time as he petitions the court for any and all changes and until such time as he completes all of the requirements as set forth in the previous mediation." [Augmented Record 127].

Commissioner Kennedy's orders on custody allow Mr. Buono to return to court as soon as the requirements are met. The requirements themselves are also minimal repairs to the home and co-parenting classes [Augmented Record 22-23].

In addition to the ambiguities in the orders themselves, the parties' conduct following the entry of these orders strongly suggest that they did not intend for these orders to be final judgments as to custody. Mr. Buono sought to modify the orders explaining that he had met the requirements to modify the temporary orders [Augmented Record 130, 149:6-15][CT 11:1-5], Mr. Buono explained that Judge Codrington's Nov. 8, 2007 orders were temporary [CT 174:1-5], and Mr. Buono repeatedly argued that Commissioner Bermudez mistakenly cancelled the trials ordered by Judge Codrington [CT 174:7-25].

Additionally, in Nov. 2007, Ms. Beggs asked that Mr. Buono be held temporarily on Professionally Supervised vitiation so that a 730-psychological evaluation could be conducted [Augmented Record 145:24-28, 146:1-8]. Further, Ms. Beggs also requested an evidentiary hearing to authenticate evidence [Augmented Record 146:1-8]. Although Ms. Beggs attorney Mr. Cohen eventually argued that the changed circumstance rule applied, he did so only after the 730 psychological evaluation recommended that Mr. Buono be taken off of supervised visitation [Confidential Material Transcript 115].

Under these circumstances, denying a Best Interest Trial would only finalize Commissioner Bermudez mistaken belief that a Final Custodial Order had been issued by Judge Codrington. And it would render Judge Codrington's interim orders Permanent and Final, ignoring Judge Codrington's own interpretation and purpose for those orders.

Therefore, Mr. Buono would request that the Appellate Court reverse and remand with a finding that there has not been a final judgement in this case, and that the Family Court used the wrong standard of review. That the correct standard was the Best Interest of the Child Standard. Further, to find that this issue has merit, such that Mr. Buono would be allowed to represent himself on remand.

III.   Did the Family Court Abuse its Discretion in Finding that there was No Change in Circumstances?

Abuse of Discretion Standard of Review

In general, "[t]he standard of appellate review of custody and visitation orders is the deferential abuse of discretion test." *(In re Marriage of Burgess (1996) 13 Cal.4th 25, 32 (Burgess).)*

"[T]he changed circumstance rule does not apply when a parent requests only a change in the parenting or visitation arrangement not amounting to a change from joint custody to sole custody, or vice versa. Instead, the trial court considers a request to change the parenting or visitation arrangement under the best interests of the child standard." *(In re Marriage of Lucio (2008) 161 Cal.App.4th 1068. 10811082.).*

However, for the purposes of this argument, we will assume that we must show a significant change of circumstances.

1.   First Change of Circumstances:

Mr. Buono was originally placed on Family Supervised Visitation on Sept. 8, 2004, because Ms. Beggs, "Suspected" that Mr. Buono was secretly bringing their child to the allegedly unrepaired family residence [Augmented Record 22-23].

However, supervised visitation was changed to professionally supervised visitation after a dispute over the Christmas 2004 visitation schedule. Specifically, there was a mistake in the custodial order which gave Ms. Beggs both Christmas Eve and Christmas Day for EVEN YEARS [Augmented Record 15]. Mr. Buono brought the error to the attention of the Family Court and the Family Court issued a verbal correction [CT 143:9-19]. However, Ms. Beggs incorrectly cited the court adjusted time schedule [CT 63:5-12]. As a result Ms. Beggs had the child for Christmas Eve [CT 63:22-25] and Mr. Buono had the child for Christmas Day [CT 64:12-13, 65:16-19].

Therein, Ms. Beggs accused Mr. Buono of intentionally withholding their child, claiming that he was an absolute danger, and that she believed that this miscommunication was a short period kidnapping [69:2-5]. And at the Jan. 6, 2005 ex-parte, Mr. Buono was placed on professionally supervised visitation. However, Ms. Beggs failed to prove any of these allegations at trial.

The findings of the Trial Court were as follows;

> "The PETITIONER shall continue with supervised visitation with a professional monitor, until such time as he petitions the court for any and all changes and until such time as he completes all of the requirements as set forth in the previous mediation." [Augmented Record 127].

And, the previous mediation required nothing more than that Mr. Buono was to complete co-parenting and to make repairs to the family home [Augmented Record 22-23]. Thus, the change of circumstance is that Mr. Buono completed co-parenting and built a brand new home in June 2005 [Augmented Record 121, 130].

2. Second Change of Circumstance:

In Nov. 2007, the Court Mediator recommended unsupervised visitation, but Ms. Beggs contested the recommendation [Augmented Record 142:11-27]. Ms. Beggs' attorney Mr. Cohen stated;

> "…Is that we really think there should be some type of psychological testing of the petitioner. … before we move to the nonmonitored. Again, we read in the papers scary things daily," [Augmented Record 145:24-28, 146:1-8].

Therein, Judge Codrington temporarily stayed unsupervised visitation [Augmented Record 153:5-7, 153:27-28, 154:1] and ordered a 730-evaluation [Augmented Record 149:20-26].

However, Dr. Suiter's 730-Evaluation recommended that Mr. Buono be taken off supervised visitation, and that Mr. Buono be placed on a step-up plan [Confidential Material Transcript 118-119]. To recite Dr. Suiter's Report;

> "In total, the data from the evaluation did not support that their son is at any risk towards being with his father. Indeed, it was noted that the child is very warm and responsive to his father and very definitely wanted to be with him…" [Confidential Material Transcript 115].

> "Further, the data does not support that he presents a risk to their son. Rather, [Mr. Buono] is likely to be quite appropriate with their son and to be focused on their son's well being. He is likely to be warm and nurturing with him as well. He is likely to engage him in age and developmental appropriate activities and is unlikely to be harsh with any disciplining."
> [Confidential Material Transcript 116].

Hence, the reason that Mr. Buono was being held temporary on supervised visitation was to allow for the 730 evaluation to be completed. The change in circumstances was when Dr. Suiter's findings showed that Mr. Buono was not a risk to the child.

3. Third Change of Circumstances:

At the Oct. 28, 2008 hearing, Commissioner Bermudez made the most critical of errors, claiming that the evidentiary hearings ordered by Judge Codrington had already been denied, appealed, and affirmed [CT 324:17-25]. This resulted in Commissioner Bermudez, on his own motion, ordering a restraining order for the child [CT 321:8-15] and a 52-week anger management for Mr. Buono [CT 323:19-21].

However, the child's restraining order has since been defeated and removed [RT 3:8-14], the 52-week anger management course completed [RT 8:14-17].

Thus, even if we assumed that all of Ms. Beggs' un-authenticated evidence had been true. Then, Mr. Buono has still overcome the additional restrictions added on by the commissioner. The change of circumstances being that these restrictions when considering Custody or Visitation have been removed.

4. Fourth Change of Circumstances:

While Ms. Beggs might have been capable of caring for the Toddler or Kindergarten aged Matthew, it appears that Ms. Beggs is struggling with the child and now teenaged Matthew. As the professional supervisor's incident report, quoted below, states;

"9/13 Minor child reported an incident that had occurred between himself and the custodial parent. Minor child stated that the custodial parent had punched him in the face during an argument that occurred in the front yard. The minor child was crying as he relayed this incident to the non-custodial parent. He stated that the custodial parent had told him that someone was coming to investigate the incident and he was scared that he might be taken away." [Confidential Material Transcript 370].

In dispute, Ms. Beggs stated,

"I believe that he is an habitual liar. I have never punched my son in the face. I am not aware of any neighbors seeing this or calling CPS on me. I have not had any visits from CPS in this regard." [CT 340:6-9].

However, the court evaluator in 2015 discovered that there had been 9-mandated calls to CPS against Ms. Beggs [Confidential Material Transcript 364-365]. Additionally, Ms. Beggs admitted that she was physically abusive toward Mr. Buono during their marriage [Augmented Record 11].

But far more concerning then Ms. Beggs action in punching the child Matthew, are Matthew's statements that Ms. Beggs had informed him that the investigator will question him, and depending upon Matthew's answers that investigator may decide to remove him from Ms. Beggs' home. Clearly, this is a pure example of coercion, convincing the child to remain silent about the physical abuse out of fear of being removed from his home.

In Dr. Suiter's 730 Psychological Evaluation it was discovered that Ms. Beggs had a the potential for losing control. To recite Dr. Suiter's Report;

"[Ms. Beggs] completed the Personality Assessment Inventory. The profile was valid. The results were reflective of an individual likely experiencing a very heightened degree of anxiety even to a degree which is unusual for clinical samples. As a result, her life is likely to be severely constricted by her tension and she may even be unable to even met minimal role expectations without feeling overwhelmed. In that regard, relatively minor stressors for her may be sufficient to result in a major crisis as she is prone to be plagued by worry making it even difficult to concentrate." [Confidential Material Transcript 110, 111]

It should be noted that Ms. Beggs denied drinking and passing out in front of the child [CT 340:10-11]. However, the child never accused Ms. Beggs of drinking in front of him, but rather, the child stated that Ms. Beggs had been 'sick' and 'hung over' [CT 172:13-14]. Noting that Court Orders had stated that Ms. Beggs was not allowed to drink alcohol in front of the child [Augmented Record 16].

Further, the professional supervisor's incident report also stated that,

"There have been times when the minor child has stated anger with the custodial parent, however he had not gone into detail. He states that the anger management that he has had in school has helped. He also states that he will be going to regular classes next year." [Confidential Material Transcript 370].

The change in circumstances rule was never meant to be a defense against child abuse. And yet, to this case, the change of circumstance rule prevents the Family Court from reading the professional supervisors incident report. It prevents the Family Court from reading the 9-CPS reports, it prevents the now 13-year-old Matthew from speaking in his own defense; meaning that while Ms. Beggs calls him a habitual liar that Matthew is not allowed to testify.

5. <u>Fifth Change of Circumstances:</u>

Ms. Beggs has been caught by the professional supervisor allowing Mr. Buono secret unsupervised visits with the child Matthew. Specifically;

- In Aug. 2013, the professional supervisor noted that approximately 40-minutes after the supervised visit had ended, that she received three phone calls from Mr. Buono and Matthew, over a 2-hour period. Wherein Matthew stated that his mother Ms. Beggs was outside, while Mr. Buono and Matthew were inside playing [Confidential Material Transcript 369].

- In June 2012, the professional supervisor noted that Ms. Beggs attended Mr. Buono's daughter's birthday party. That Ms. Beggs sat at the same table as Mr. Buono, that Ms. Beggs sang happy birthday, ate cake, and watched Mr. Buono's daughter opened presents.

- Also, in June 2012, the professional supervisor noted that after the supervised visitation had ended that Ms. Beggs took the child back into the birthday party unsupervised [Confidential Material Transcript 369].

Clearly, if Ms. Beggs can attend birthday parties, sitting at the same table, eating cake, and singing with Mr. Buono. If Ms. Beggs can bring their child to parties unsupervised, and leave their child Matthew alone with Mr. Buono for hours at a time. Then Ms. Beggs is capable of exchanging the teenaged Matthew once or twice a week for an unsupervised visit.

A minimal change from supervised visitation to unsupervised visitation would likely only reduce Ms. Beggs' burden. We realize that Ms. Beggs' and the Supervisor's schedules do not always fit, causing the visitation schedule to be random, with the days and times continually changing, sometimes the visits are simply cancelled or never scheduled for that week. The result is a child who has no idea if he will see his father on any given week.

Additionally, Matthew is now in junior high, thus Matthew would benefit from visitations that include homework and tutoring time. While Ms. Beggs resents the idea of visitations that occur while Ms. Beggs is at work nights and weekends. Denying the teenager these benefits on the grounds that there is no change in circumstances is beyond unreasonable.

Therefore, Mr. Buono would request that the Appellate Court reverse and remand with a finding that there has been a showing of a significant change of circumstances. And that this issue has merit such that Mr. Buono would be allowed to represent himself on remand.

CONCLUSION

First, Mr. Buono's OSC sought 12-hours of unsupervised visitation [CT 172:6-10]. Noting that Mr. Buono already had 12-hours of professionally supervised visitations [Augmented Record 153:5-15]. And Mr. Buono has been consistently visiting their son for over 12-years, with all visits being successful and uneventful [Confidential Material Transcript 366-370]. Therein, Mr. Buono is not seeking additional time with his child. He merely seeks an adjustment in the terms of visitation. The only change that will result from the court's order is that Mr. Buono will be able to visit his child alone, without the intrusion of expense of a third party supervisor.

Mr. Buono's requested alterations to the existing parenting and visitation schedules would not have created a de facto joint custody arrangement. *(See In re Marriage of Biallas (1998) 65 Cal.App.4th 755, 760, 76 Cal.Rptr.2d 717* [when father has right to visit on alternate weekends and one weeknight each week, custody was not joint custody].) The requested alterations would not disrupt the children's established patterns of care and emotional bonds with Ms. Beggs or destabilize the sole physical custody arrangement. As in Enrique M., Mr. Buono's proposed changes to the visitation schedule, though altering the parenting schedule, were not "on par with a request to change physical custody from sole to joint custody, or vice versa." *(Enrique M., supra, 121 Cal.App.4th at p. 1382, 18 Cal.Rptr.3d 306.)*

"[T]he changed circumstance rule does not apply when a parent requests only a change in the parenting or visitation arrangement not amounting to a change from joint custody to sole custody, or vice versa. Instead, the trial court considers a request to change the parenting or visitation arrangement under the best interests of the child standard." *(In re Marriage of Lucio (2008) 161 Cal.App.4th 1068. 10811082.).*

However, on Aug. 4, 2016, Commissioner Dickerson denied the motion stating;

> "… It's a Montenegro order. There is no material change of circumstances. … I just agree with Mr. Cohen. -- this case goes so far back … So it's an old case. I can't go back and rehash 13 years of history. I can only rule on what I have today, and I just don't find a material change of circumstances. There is no change. [RT 12:15-27].

Second, in our case, there does not appear to be a 'Final Custodial Order' The final judgment, was issued May 19, 2005 [CT 429], but was not signed until Mar. 28, 2006 [Augmented Record 124]. The final judgment states in relevant part that,

> "The PETITIONER shall continue with supervised visitation with a professional monitor, until such time as he petitions the court for any and all changes and until such time as he completes all of the requirements as set forth in the previous mediation." [Augmented Record 127].

And, the previous mediation required nothing more than that Mr. Buono was to complete co-parenting and to make repairs to the family home [Augmented Record 22-23]. The co-parenting was completed in Mar. 2005 [Augmented Record 121], Mr. Buono built a brand new home in June 2005 [Augmented Record 121, 130].

Thereafter, Judge Codrington ordered a Temporary Custodial Order;

"… As an interim order I would like to increase that time…" "And I see by your reaction, ma'am, you don't want to increase the time, but I am staying the unsupervised visits and giving Father up to 12 hours per week," [Augmented Record 153:5-7, 153:27-28, 154:1].

And then, at the Oct. 28, 2008 Trial, Commissioner Bermudez made the most critical of errors, as Commissioner Bermudez claimed that the evidentiary hearings ordered by Judge Codrington had already been denied, appealed, and affirmed. To recite Commissioner Bermudez;

"I scratch my head, gentlemen, because it appears that Judge Codrington in 2007 ruled that there weren't any change circumstances. Her ruling was challenged. The Court of Appeals sustained her ruling, so I wonder if there are any changed circumstances even in the pleading that are before me. … you would have the burden to tell me your changed circumstances." [CT 324:17-25].

Commissioner Bermudez's final comments before dismissing the motion;

"For the record, number one, as I indicated in my opening comments to both of you gentlemen, it seems to me this issue has already been addressed not once but twice. Both times no change were found. I would be prepared to find there aren't changed circumstances at this point warranting a revisitation of the parenting time between the parties." [CT 334:3-14].

Under these circumstances, denying a Best Interest Trial would only finalize Commissioner Bermudez mistaken belief that a Final Custodial Order had been issued by Judge Codrington. And it would render Judge Codrington's interim orders Permanent and Final, ignoring Judge Codrington's own interpretation and purpose for those orders.

Third, Ms. Beggs' ability to care for the toddler or kindergartener Matthew may have stratified the courts in 2008 and 2009. But clearly, Ms. Beggs is having difficulty maintaining a proper environment for the teenager Matthew.

The professional supervisor's incident report tells us that;

> "9/13 Minor child reported an incident that had occurred between himself and the custodial parent. Minor child stated that the custodial parent had punched him in the face during an argument that occurred in the front yard. The minor child was crying as he relayed this incident to the non-custodial parent. He stated that the custodial parent had told him that someone was coming to investigate the incident and he was scared that he might be taken away." [Confidential Material Transcript 370].

In dispute Ms. Beggs argued that;

> "I believe that he is an habitual liar. I have never punched my son in the face. I am not aware of any neighbors seeing this or calling CPS on me. I have not had any visits from CPS in this regard." [CT 340:6-9].

However, the court evaluator in 2015 discovered that there had been 9-mandated calls to CPS against Ms. Beggs [Confidential Material Transcript 364-365].

The change in circumstances rule was never meant to be a defense against child abuse. And yet, to this case, the change of circumstance rule prevents the Family Court from looking into any of the details of these allegations. Ms. Beggs is absolutely allowed to call the teenager Matthew a habitual liar, saying that he is lying about being physically beaten by her, but the teenager is not allowed to testify in his own defense.

Further, the minimal change from supervised visitation to unsupervised visitation would reduce Ms. Beggs' household burden. We realize that Ms. Beggs' and the Supervisor's schedules do not always fit, causing the visitation schedule to be random, with the days and times continually changing, sometimes the visits are simply cancelled or never scheduled for that week. The result is a child (now teenager) who has no idea if he will see his father on any given week.

Therefore, Mr. Buono would request that the Appellate Court reverse and remand with a finding amicable to the arguments presented within this brief. That Mr. Buono was either not required to show a change of circumstance because the motion was limited to a request for visitation, or because there had not been a final judgement. Or that a significant change of circumstances has been shown. To these arguments, that the Family Court must proceed in consideration of the Child's Best Interest. And that this issue has merit to allow Mr. Buono to represent himself on remand.

Respectfully Submitted,

by _____

Salvatore A. Buono

CERTIFICATE OF COMPLIANCE

Pursuant to rule 14 (c) of the California Rules of Court. I hereby certify that this brief contains 12,910 words, no foot notes. In making this certification, I have relied on the word count of the computer program used to prepare the brief.

By *Teresa Dooley*

Teresa Dooley